An Inspector Calls: The Ultimate Audio Revision Guide

By

D1826062

Emily Bird

And

Jeff Thomas

The Inspector

You'll never know where I come from,
Just focus on my function.
Even though you're not in the play,
My message applies to you today.

1

I'd like to ask some questions,
using the power of suggestion.
I'll draw confession from you hearts,
using psychological arts.
Divide and conquer, that's my way,
I work on a hunch and hearsay.

2

When you're at the height of smugness,
I'll inform you of the girl's death.
I will stress the pain she suffered,
watch you close, see if you're bothered.
One line of enquiry at a time,
To see who's guilty of this crime.

3

First I question Mr Birling,
all part of strategic planning.
First bring down the most senior man,
this upsets the rest of the clan.
I make him squirm, I make him mad,
but he won't admit he's done bad.

4

Next I turn to the most fragile,
it's Sheila's turn to be on trial.
She breaks down, admits her guilt
but from tears, moral fibre is built.
Stronger now than ever before,
she'll help me win this war.

5

Now it's Gerald's turn to confess,
claims he saw Daisy in distress.
At the end of his sad story,
I mention I read her diary.
I use this 'proof' to show him up,
rub in the pain of their break up.

6

Then I turn to Mrs Birling,
pride and conceit is her failing.
At first I let her rant and rave,
then lead her to her social grave.
Hoisted by her own petard,
a guilty son is her reward.

7

I left the worst person 'til last,
Eric has to admit what's passed.
Like his sister, Eric rises,
agrees with me, there must
be changes.
As things start to fall apart,
I make one last speech then depart.

Coda:

Observe and learn
we're all entwined.
Observe and learn
to save mankind.

Explore the tactics used by Inspector Goole in order to extract the truth from his suspects?

Introduction

- Make an opening statement about Goole's tactics.

Goole's Tactics

- Divide and conquer - he interrogates characters one by one, making them vulnerable so it is easier to get their confession. "**One line of inquiry at a time.**" Act 1
- Use of 'evidence' such as the photographs - legitimises his accusations. "**She recognized her from the photograph, didn't she?**" Act 1
- He repeats the images of the girl dying a horrible, painful death - plays upon the characters' emotions. "**she'd swallowed a lot of strong disinfectant. Burnt her insides out, of course.**" Act 1
- He uses a direct and persistent questioning style - does not allow the suspects to divert the inquiry. "**Who is to blame then?**" Act 2
- He often cuts other characters off while they're talking - controls what the other characters get to say. "**(cutting in, sharply) We do need him here.**" Act 2
- Asks leading questions - gives the impression he already knows. "**You admit to being prejudiced against her case?**" Act 2

Conclusion

- Sum up how effective you believe Goole's tactics to be in terms of making the other characters admit their guilt.

Vocabulary: commanding, controlled, disciplined, dominant, eerie, humanitarian, incisive, passionate, uncanny, unnerving

Mr Birling

I never take responsibility,
I have dreams of being nobility.
I never accept responsibility,
Force me and you'll meet hostility.

1

So pleased with life on
this special evening,
a wedding will secure
business dealings.
Sheila will wed into
a better class,
this will give you
some kudos at last.

2

So full of advice you
make a long speech,
no strikes, no war
are what you preach.
Strikes are brewing
but your head's in the sand,
war is looming but
you don't understand.

3

So self absorbed you boast of
your graces,
of titles you've held and
friends in high places
but inside you're still a
provincial guy,
once the Inspector arrives
your power will die.

4

So intent on being a
strong business man,
wage increases are not
part of your plan.
Faced with a strike you
took practical steps,
a few sackings are what
the industry expects.

5

So confident that
your actions are right,
when accused of a crime
you put up a fight.
Despite this strong stance,
you're starting to shake,
so when focus shifts,
you're glad of the break.

6

So full of fear that there'll
be a big scandal,
you offer thousands to
avoid going to trial.
To avoid your guilt
you admonish your son,
you rebuke the rest,
the reproaches have begun.

7

So frantic for escape,
you start to suppose,
it was a hoax is what
you propose.
When Gerald confirms
your new suspicion,
you revert back to
your old position.

8

So full of relief,
you think danger's passed,
you laugh at your children,
you complacence is vast.
But just when you think it
will all be fine,
an inspector's announced for
the second time.

How does Priestley ensure that the audience finds Mr Birling an unpleasant character?

Introduction

- Make an opening statement about why is it important that the audience sees Mr Birling as unpleasant.

Birling's unpleasant characteristics

- Drinks the same port as Lord Croft - trying to be someone he is not. "**Finchley told me it's exactly the same port your father gets**" Act 1
- Gives long, boring speeches - makes him seem full of self importance. "**Just le me finish, Eric**" Act 1
- Dismisses world troubles - makes him look ignorant. "**I say there isn't a chance of war**" Act 1
- Name drops about powerful people he knows - makes him look both boastful and insecure. "**How do you get on with our Chief Constable, Colonel Roberts?... I ought to warn you that he's an old friend of mine**" Act 1
- Won't accept that he acted badly towards Eva, saying he was in line with industry standards - makes him look callous. "**We were paying the usual rates**" Act 1
- Berates his family for their confessions - makes him look unsupportive. "**why you all had to go letting everything come out like that, beats me**" Act 3

Conclusion

- Sum up why Priestley made Mr Birling such an unappealing character.

Vocabulary: bombastic, greedy, ignorant, oblivious, overbearing, pompous, provincial, uncouth, unrepentant, verbose

Sheila Birling

I lived in a dream but now I've awoken,
I'm looking at life with eyes wide open.
I've heeded the words that were spoken.

1
I'll take you back to the
evening in question,
the toil of others went
without mention.
All we thought of was
clothes and champagne,
my coming marriage,
material gain.

2
I'll tell you that,
even then I was troubled,
suspicions of Gerald
had kept me puzzled.
I wondered where he'd
been all last summer,
but I knew deep down
he'd loved with another.

3
I'll tell you that when
I saw the ring,
the misgivings I'd had,
started to sink.
To be Mrs Croft just
filled me with bliss,
to snub Gerald's offer
would seem so amiss.

4
I'll admit that when
I met the Inspector,
earlier happiness
started to falter.
First he exposed my father
as heartless,
then he revealed how I'd
been so callous.

5
I couldn't believe the
tale that was told,
I suddenly realised that
I was involved.
Driven by envy,
I'd got her sacked,
shame and regret followed
my act.

6
I felt so bad,
my thoughts in a whirl,
then Gerald betrayed
that he'd loved the girl.
I urged him to tell,
just to come clean,
he thought that I was
just being mean.

7
I wasn't trying to cause
any strife,
but he thought I enjoyed
twisting the knife.
I needed to see it wasn't
just me,
who had to take
responsibility.

8
I can never go back to
the girl that I was,
Goole showed me the problems
that are now my cause.
The world is changing
and so am I,
no longer naïve or
willing to lie.

Trace the development of Sheila's relationship with Gerald to revise how her character changes.

Introduction

- Explain that Sheila becomes more mature during the play and this affects her relationship with Gerald.

Development of Sheila

- At the beginning, she's excited about being engaged. **"I think it's perfect. Now I really feel engaged."** Act 1
- Sheila has suspicions about Gerald. **"during that time when you hardly came near me."** Act 1
- Sheila admits her part in the scandal, showing she is accepting responsibility, but also wants Gerald to do the same. **"All right, Gerald, you needn't look at me like that. At least, I'm trying to tell the truth, I expect you've done things you're ashamed of too."** Act 1
- During the revelations Sheila begins to stand up to Gerald and question him, showing she is becoming his equal. **"Then why say I want to see somebody else put through it?"** Act 2
- At the end Sheila neither accepts or rejects Gerald's re-proposal, showing she is not in awe of him like she was at the beginning. **"No, not yet, it's too soon. I must think."** Act 3

Conclusion

- Sum up the fact that Sheila becomes stronger during the play and this makes her more circumspect about her engagement to Gerald.

Vocabulary: compassionate, contrite, honest, intelligent, jealous, mature, naive, perceptive, reformed, supportive

Gerald Croft

What a catch:
Handsome, rich and blest,
But there's a catch
You're as guilty as the rest.

1

At first glance I'm the
hero of the play,
easy are the manners
that I display.
Sheila's in love and
Birling's in awe,
but beneath my good
looks exists a flaw.

2

All it takes is to
mention Renton's name,
I betray myself, Sheila
sees my shame.
Soon it emerges I'd
had an affair,
no place to hide, in
the guilt I must share.

3

A bad day at work,
a night at the bar,
Daisy was there,
I was her saviour.
Rescued her from a
life on the street,
she became my mistress
and source of deceit.

4

I let her live in my
friend's empty flat,
but only until he
needed it back.
She thought she had found
true love, real joy,
but really she was just
a rich man's toy.

5

So was I the best or
was I the worst?
Six months of bliss
I gave her at first
but I broke her heart
and cast her aside,
wasn't this the main
reason why she died?

6

So pleased with myself
when I reveal the hoax,
I can return to my
drinks and my jokes.
At the end of the play I've
not learnt a thing,
I expect Sheila to take
back the ring.

Is Gerald a hero or a villain?

Introduction

- Gerald has both high and low points during the play. Decide what your attitudes is towards his status as a hero or villain and put this into a sentence.

Gerald as a hero

- Gerald gets engaged to Sheila even though his parents don't approve, suggesting he is marrying her for love. "**I insist upon being one of the family now. I've been trying long enough, haven't I?**" Act 1
- Gerald says that when he first met Daisy, he was saving her from Alderman Meggarty. "**Old Joe Meggarty, half-drunk and goggle-eyed, had wedged her into a corner**" Act 2

Gerald as a villain

- Gerald has an affair with Daisy. "**when we met again - not accidentally this time of course**" Act 2
- Gerald ends the affair with Daisy when the free accommodation runs out. "**set her up as his mistress and then dropped her when it suited him.**" Act 2
- Gerald behaves as if he's learnt nothing and even expects Sheila to reaccept his engagement ring. "**Everything's all right now, Sheila. What about this ring?**" Act 3

Conclusion

- After adding in further arguments of your own, sum up whether Gerald is a hero or a villain.

Vocabulary: ashamed, cheat, conservative, ignorant, inquisitive, privileged, remorseless, selfish, smug, traditional

Mrs Birling – Mother Inferior

You think you're the best
You act so superior.
But you're so cold
You're the mother inferior.

You're fixed in role as wife
and strict mother,
any bad manners you
instantly smother.
Reproach your husband
for thanking the cook,
scold Sheila's bad language
and give her a look.

You accept your place
as second to men,
business is more important
now and then.
You tutor your daughter
to think the same way,
she mustn't tease Gerald
when he plays away.

When you hear of the
girl and her sad death,
you sound snobbish
and cruel all in one breath.
Your daughter tries to
give you good counsel,
you dismiss her advice
of being more humble.

When talking to Goole
you act high and mighty,
think you're in control,
show you're not sorry.
You boast of position,
tell him he's rude,
he puts you in a very
aggressive mood.

Then the truth starts flow,
you're shocked to the core,
your little boy's not
innocent anymore.
You thought he was sweet,
but now he's a let-down,
out drinking with seedy
girls of the town.

Let's never forget your
charity work,
but this specific case
made you feel irked.
The girl in distress
called herself Birling,
so you refused any help
and left her wanting.

You never back down,
never say sorry,
family reputation is
your only worry.
To relieve hidden guilt
you call for justice,
you blame the young man
who's been so feckless.

You realise too late
you've blamed your own son,
because of you pride
your woe's just begun.
Just like your husband
you never learn,
a bad role model for
the audience to spurn.

Is it fair to label Mrs Birling as a snob?

Introduction

- Decide if you think it is fair to label Mrs Birling as a snob, but also take into account her other characteristics and the historical context.

Mrs Birling's snobbish attitude

- Mrs Birling feels that she is socially superior to her husband. Regarding compliments to the cook, "**Arthur, you're not supposed to say such things**" Act 1
- She feels superior to Goole and demonstrates this through her haughty attitude. "**I must say that so far you seem to be conducting it in a rather peculiar and offensive manner**" Act 2
- She questions what Gerald says about Alderman Meggarty because she believes the upper classes should be beyond reproach. "**surely you don't mean Alderman Meggarty?**" Act 2
- She believes that working class people have loose morals. "**I don't suppose for a moment that we can understand why the girl committed suicide. Girls of that class -**" Act 2
- Doesn't learn anything from Goole's visit. "**In the morning they'll be as amused as we are.**" Act 3

Conclusion

- Sum up your opinion, have you been able to make a case that shows Mrs Birling is a snob?

Vocabulary: cold, condescending, controlling, haughty, imperious, judgemental, snobbish, proud, uncaring, unreformed

Eric Birling – Disconnected

Hello Father,
it's Eric calling...
Father I know, that I've
let you down.
Stole from you,
when you weren't around,
but never forget,
I'm ashamed of you too.
Reputation can't
rule all that you do.
If only we'd been close –
like father and son,
but just like now,
you never listen.
Father always hangs up on me.

Hello Mother,
it's Eric calling...
Mother I know that
I've brought you shame,
but you were so quick
to pass me the blame.
I'm sorry I'm not your
good little boy,
but you stifled my life,
killed all the joy.
If only we'd been close –
like mother and son,
but just like now,
you never listen.
Mother always hangs up on me.

Hello Sheila,
it's Eric calling...
Sheila I know that
we weren't that close,
but after what happened
I need you the most.
Just like me you
saw change was needed,

you listened to Goole,
his words were heeded.
It's our job to fight for
those like Eva,
to bring about justice,
make the world fairer.
Sheila always listens to me.

Hello Daisy,
it's Eric calling...
I will say sorry
a thousand times
but it's never enough
to erase my crimes.
I took advantage,
forced my way in,
I was so drunk,
I don't remember my sin.
I tried to support
the baby and you
but stolen money just
made us argue.
Daisy's ghost can't hear me.

Hello Inspector,
it's Eric calling...
Inspector I know
I behaved badly.
I will make amends,
I'll do it gladly.
Your visit was harsh
it taught me a lesson.
Now your words have
become my mission.
So follow my lead,
look to your neighbour,
they're real people,
not just cheap labour.
The Inspector smiles and nods.

Is Eric an immoral character?

Introduction

- Eric exhibits lots of undesirable behaviour, however, not all of it is immoral.

Eric's behaviour

- Eric makes comments about Sheila during the dinner. **"She's got a nasty temper sometimes"** Act 1. However, this is merely indiscreet rather than immoral.
- Eric admits that he collected in small accounts at his father's office. **"There were some small accounts to collect, and I asked for cash"** Act 3. Here, he lied and embezzled his father's company, however, this immoral behaviour was done in order to support Daisy.
- During his interrogation Eric explains that he threatened to cause a disturbance if Daisy wouldn't let him go back to her lodgings. **"I threatened to make a row"** Act 3. By forcing himself into her life, Eric was acting in an immoral way.
- At the end he says that he, and his mother are mainly to blame for Daisy's death. **"You lot may be letting yourselves out nicely but I can't. Nor can mother."**
- At the end, Eric says he is ashamed of his parents' behaviour and attitudes. **"I'm ashamed of your as well - yes both of you."** Act 3 This shows he's learnt to distinguish between moral and immoral behaviour.

Conclusion

- Give a balanced summation of Eric's character after looking at all the evidence.

Vocabulary: amoral, ashamed, contrite, immature, indiscreet, irresponsible, reckless, rueful, thoughtless, unprincipled

Eva and Priestley – My Silent Siren

My silent siren,
A warning to us all.
My silent siren,
Will they listen to your call?

1
I'm going to make you
pretty but beware,
there's a lot of jealousy
out there.
I'm going to make you
pretty but beware,
there are a lot of
predators out there.

2
In the trenches I saw
so much pain,
I witnessed so many men
killed in vain.
Brothers in war, men
fought side by side
but after, still judged
by the class divide.

3
I'm going to give you
spirit but take heed,
it won't protect you from
their greed.
I'm going to give you
spirit but take heed,
it won't help you in your
hour of need.

4
I vowed that the world
would have to adjust,
to be based on respect
and mutual trust.
I sent the script to
a communist state,
seeing the play, Russians
thought it was great.

5
I'm going to craft you
cryptic but look out,
it will throw your
killers into doubt.
I'm going to craft you
cryptic but look out,
responsibility they
will still flout.

What techniques does Priestley use to make Eva an appealing character?

Introduction

- Observe that it is necessary for Eva/Daisy to be an appealing character in order to draw the audience into the narrative on an emotional level.

Techniques

- Her youth is mentioned several times, and makes her death more poignant as she never has the chance to fulfil her potential. **"Two hours ago a young woman died in the Infirmary."** Act 1
- She is innocent of any wrong-doing, the audience can see she did not deserve to be punished in any way. **"Eva Smith lost her job with Birling and Company because the strike failed and they were determined not to have another one."** Act 1
- Her prettiness is emphasized many times, which is essential in attracting the attention of both Gerald and Eric, as well as Sheila's jealousy. This in turn shows that she was punished for reasons beyond her control. **"If she'd been some miserable plain little creature, I don't suppose I'd have done it."** Act 1
- She has high moral standards and won't accept money from Eric once she knows it's stolen. **"She wouldn't take any more"** Act 3

Conclusion

- Sum up the techniques and their effects.

Vocabulary: desperate, innocent, moral, mysterious, pretty, spirited, symbolic, young, unhappy, vulnerable

The Structure of "An Inspector Calls"

An Inspector calls at the start of the play,
Even when he's left the problems still stay.
An Inspector calls at the end of the play,
History's repeating, it won't go away.

1
Why does it start with
a happy party?
Because this makes their
fall all the more mighty.
To go from sheer joy to
the depths of despair,
plus it's the reason
all suspects are there.

2
What do we know before
Goole arrives?
How they behave in their
ordinary lives.
Birling's a bore and
Sheila feels a doubt,
now we are ready to
watch them fall out.

3
How does Goole structure
his enquiries?
One crime at a time
to beguile and tease.
This keeps the audience
on their toes.
Step by careful step
is how the play goes.

4
Why do we have three
different Acts?
To allow cliff-hangers,
you can't relax.
First Gerald's guilty face,
then Eric's doom,
leave us eager for the
play to resume.

5
Why does Goole leave
before the play is done?
It gives the others time
to discuss his sermon.
The audience can see who
has learned what.
Who is ready to change
and who is not.

6
Why do we have the
final phone call?
They haven't got away,
they're about to fall.
They thought is was a
hoax and they were okay
but misery and guilt are
on their way.

Investigate what happens at the beginning and end of each act to explore the structure of the play.

Introduction
- The beginning and end of each act is structured in order to maintain high levels of tension.

Act 1
- Beginning - The family are having the engagement party, but cracks are beginning to show. "**Except for all last summer, when you never came near me**"
- End - Cliff hanger as Sheila prompts Gerald to reveal his involvement with Eva. "**you knew her very well**"

Act 2
- Beginning - Gerald evades revealing his involvement in front of Sheila. "**Why stay when you'll hate it?**"
- End - Mrs Birling realises that she's condemned her own son. "**I don't believe it. I *won't* believe it**"

Act 3
- Beginning - Eric returns to discover that his secrets are out. He takes responsibility and explains his story.
- End - A telephone call signals the whole process is about to start again. "**a police inspector is on his way**"

Conclusion
- Conclude how the open and close of each act works to maintain high levels of tension.

Vocabulary: act, aftermath, baseline, climax, finale, interval, legacy, revelations, suspense, tension

The Language of "An Inspector Calls"

Though she's the focus,
Daisy can't speak,
a working class girl
who's words would sound weak.
Instead of her voice
we have the Inspector,
a powerful man gives
weight to the lecture.

Light-hearted with
jokes at the start of the play,
Sheila rags Gerald
about staying away
but many a true word
is said in jest,
and she finds the truth
is just as she'd guessed.

When the talk turns
to a taboo theme,
euphemisms are used,
a linguistic screen,
a phrase you'll hear
is "women of the town",
because words like prostitute
bring the tone down.

The language is posh,
the language is old,
idioms help the story unfold.
"Sounds a bit fishy" can
leave us perplexed,
but these old sayings
help set the context.

Sheila grows stronger
throughout the play,
at first her words show
she's keen to obey,
but when the Inspector
has opened her eyes,
her words become challenging,
passionate cries.

Gerald's turn comes,
he's ashamed to confess,
doesn't want Sheila to hear
of his mess.
He tries to send his
fiancée away,
so she cannot hear
what he has to say.

Language is power,
a means of control,
keep their names from
the press is Birling's goal.
He's just concerned
about keeping his name,
hushing up quiet his
family's shame.

Look at the tone and
the way words are said,
emotions run high due
to fear and dread.
Tempers are lost,
and tensions rise,
for the guilt and the
shame there's no disguise.

How does Priestley use language to enhance the play?

Introduction

- Priestley uses a range of language techniques in order to enhance the play.

Language

- Edwardian idioms help to root the play in its historical context. **"Steady the Buffs!"** Act 1
- Jokes have serious undertones. **(*half serious, half playful*) Yes - except for all last summer"** Act 1
- Characters incriminate themselves through verbal reactions. **"she changed her name to Daisy Renton - GERALD (*startled*) What?"** Act 1
- The characters use euphemisms when they want or need to talk about subjects that are considered taboo. **"women of the town"** Act 2
- Narrative speeches are used to explain involvement in the case. **"She looked young and fresh..."** Act 2
- Questions prompt confessions and draw out details. **"Come along, Mr Croft. What happened?"** Act 2
- Emotive language is used to engage both the characters and the audience. **"each of you helped to kill her"** Act 3

Conclusion

- The language techniques enhance the impact and emotional depth of the play.

Vocabulary: crescendo, demands, euphemisms, implied, idioms, narratives, questions, secrets, teasing, tone

Historical Context
The Great Unrest

In the grip of The Great Unrest,
Strikes and riots and suffrage protest.
On the brink of two World Wars,
Death and conflict and working class poor.

Written at the end of
World War Two,
horrors of war,
the audience knew.
But cleverly set before
The Great War,
when the trouble had
just begun.

In Europe the war
was brewing,
but Birling couldn't see
it happening .
Responsibility was
brushed aside,
as a result millions died.

Miners started to
demand more pay,
seven hours work
maximum each day.
More workers followed
the miners' lead,
but often these appeals
did not succeed.

Cars and planes were
being improved,
but the poor from this
fun were far removed.
Birling boasted
of the Titanic,
but in the Atlantic
an iceberg sunk it.

Socialism was fast
on the rise,
H.G. Wells tried to
open people's eyes.
But men like Birling
said he was a crank,
they feared socialism
would break their bank.

Women were demanding
suffrage,
to break free from
the domestic cage.
This created more
social unrest,
as men felt only they
knew what was best.

Why is the historical context a key aspect of the play?

Introduction

- Priestley set the play in a specific era in order to make key points about society and human behaviour.

Historical Context

- The play is set in 1912, during the Edwardian Era.
- In 1912, countries such as Egypt and India were part of the British Empire. By the time the play was written, the Empire was beginning to decline.
- In April 1912, the Titanic sank on its maiden voyage.
- During the Edwardian Era, groups such as the miners went on strike to try and get better pay and conditions.
- Many people campaigned to secure votes for women.
- Edwardian Britain had a rigid class system, where the upper class were largely in control and the working class were often exploited.
- New technology was being developed during the Edwardian Era, with innovations in transport of particular interest.
- In 1924, Ramsay MacDonald became the first Labour Prime Minister.
- Between when the play is set (1912) and when it was written (1946), Britain had endured two world wars.

Conclusion

- Priestley uses the historical context to suggest that society still had a lot to learn.

Vocabulary: class, Edwardian, empire, Labour, socialism, strikes, suffragettes, technology, Titanic, war

It's better if you revise together

Try getting your friends and family involved in your revision so that you can try out some of these drama based revision activities…

- Imagine that Daisy's case has gone to court, take on the role of a judge and perform giving out punishments. *What punishments would the judge like to hand out? How might these be different from what characters can be convicted of based on hard evidence?*

- Take on the role of Daisy, and act out her meeting the other characters at the end of the play. *What would she like to say to the others? What emotions would be apparent, how would the characters react to her?*

- Put each character in the 'hot-seat' and question them about their motives and behaviour. *What does this tell you about their motives?*

- Create tableaux for key moments in the play, for instance: when Gerald gives Sheila the engagement ring, when Mrs Birling realises she's condemned her own son or right at the end of the play when Mr Birling announces that another police inspector is on his way. *Where would characters be standing/sitting in relation to each other? What expressions would be on their faces and why?*

- Recreate the past scenes that the characters describe in their confessions, for instance: Sheila complaining about Eva at Milwards, Mrs Birling interviewing Daisy at the charity committee, or Gerald telling Daisy that she has to leave the flat. *Does this make you more or less sympathetic to the characters and their original actions?*

- Create a sketch where Lord and Lady Croft try to talk Gerald out of marrying Sheila. *Why do they object to the marriage and why does Gerald want to go through with it?*

- Create an extra scene to go at the end of the play to explore how the characters react to hearing that another policeman is on his way. *Would Mr and Mrs Birling go back into a panic again? Would they try and concoct a story to cover up the truth? Would Sheila and Eric be determined to tell the truth or persuaded to keep quiet?*

Useful exam tips... a few pointers that might help:

- Work smarter not harder: listen to the guide as often as possible, for example when walking to school or doing your paper round. This is dead time that can be used effectively to really get to know the facts.

- Get someone to test you.

- Know which exam board and which texts you are using. I know this sounds obvious, but exam papers sometimes have lots of different option choices in one paper. Only do the questions on the texts you have studied for.

- Never waffle. Just answer the question. Don't assume more writing equals more marks.

- Look at as many past papers as possible before the big day. Get to know the style of questions you are likely to be asked.

- Download our model answers and read over them several times, to really get to know them.

- Practice writing your own responses to these questions and then compare.

- Use the exam board mark schemes and grade the model essays to see where they've met the requirements.

- If at first you feel you don't know the answer to a question, leave it and come back to it. Build your confidence by answering the questions you know well first. Remember you can answer the questions in any order.

- Learn your key words, as spelling is important.

About us...

Jeff Thomas

Until recently, Jeff worked as a history teacher, specialising in alternative teaching methods. Jeff has also worked alongside the University of Sussex in the role of PGCE mentor, and has trained numerous student teachers. With the ever growing success of Revision Rocks, Jeff has now stopped teaching, in order to work full-time on developing new and exciting revision aids. Jeff also works as an expert examiner for Edexcel.

Jeff has appeared on: BBC 5 live, BBC Sussex, Kent, London and Surrey to talk about cutting edge revision techniques and Revision Rocks. Jeff has also been featured in the Times Educational Supplement (TES) on two occasions, in relation to revising through song. Jeff has also made many radio appearances for the BBC to discuss issues relating to history and secondary education, which he says makes him feel very important within the world of teaching.

Emily Bird

Emily trained as an English teacher, but has also taught other subjects including: History, Psychology and R.E. Emily developed her teaching career in the area of SEN, and has a great deal of experience in working with dyslexic and autistic pupils. Emily worked with the University of Brighton as a Professional Tutor and mentor to trainee teachers. Over the years, Emily has been a regular examiner for AQA. Emily now works full time on writing material and adding to the Revision Rocks range.

©Revision Rocks 2011-7. The copyright of these sound recordings is owned by Emily Bird and Jeff Thomas. All rights reserved. This guide is designed for home use and cannot be copied or downloaded onto school websites/learning platforms without the consent of Revision Rocks. Published by Revision Rocks, Mundesley, England.

Customer satisfaction guaranteed: We want you to be entirely happy with our products. If for any reason there is a problem, please contact us directly: jeff.thomas@revisionrocks.co.uk and we promise to solve the issue.